'HE l'~'''

CARYL CHURCHILL

Caryl Churchill has written for the stage, television and radio.
Her stage plays include *Owners* (Royal Court Theatre Upstairs,
1972); *Objections to Sex and Violence* (Royal Court, 1975); *Light Shining
in Buckinghamshire* (Joint Stock on tour incl. Royal Court Upstairs,
1976, revived at National Theatre, 2015); *Vinegar Tom* (Monstrous
Regiment on tour, incl. Half Moon and ICA, 1976); *Traps* (Royal
Court Upstairs, 1977); *Cloud Nine* (Joint Stock on tour incl. Royal
Court, 1979, then Theatre de Lys, New York, 1981); *Three More
Sleepless Nights* (Soho Poly and Royal Court Upstairs, 1980); *Top Girls*
(Royal Court, then Public Theater, New York, 1982); *Fen* (Joint
Stock on tour, incl. Almeida and Royal Court, then Public Theater,
New York, 1983); *Softcops* (RSC at the Pit, 1984); *A Mouthful of Birds*
with David Lan (Joint Stock on tour, incl. Royal Court, 1986);
Serious Money (Royal Court and Wyndham's, London, then Public
Theater, New York, 1987); *Icecream* (Royal Court, 1989); *Mad Forest*
(Central School of Speech and Drama, then Royal Court, 1990);
Lives of the Great Poisoners with Orlando Gough and Ian Spink
(Second Stride on tour, incl. Riverside Studios, London, 1991); *The
Skriker* (Royal National Theatre, 1994, revived at Royal Exchange,
Manchester, 2015); *Thyestes* translated from Seneca (Royal Court
Upstairs, 1994); *Hotel* with Orlando Gough and Ian Spink (Second
Stride on tour, incl. The Place, London, 1997); *This is a Chair*
(London International Festival of Theatre at the Royal Court,
1997); *Blue Heart* (Joint Stock on tour, incl. Royal Court, 1997); *Far
Away* (Royal Court Upstairs, 2000, and Albery, London, 2001, then
New York Theatre Workshop, 2002); *A Number* (Royal Court
Downstairs, 2002, then New York Theatre Workshop, 2004,
revived at Nuffield, Southampton, 2014, then Young Vic, London,
2015); *A Dream Play* after Strindberg (Royal National Theatre,
2005); *Drunk Enough to Say I Love You?* (Royal Court Downstairs,
2006, then Public Theater, New York, 2008); *Bliss* translated from
Olivier Choinière (Ro
– *a play for Gaza* (Royal
Court Theatre Downs
Court Theatre Downs

Caryl Churchill

HERE WE GO

NICK HERN BOOKS

London

www.nickhernbooks.co.uk

A Nick Hern Book

Here We Go first published in Great Britain as a paperback original in 2015 by Nick Hern Books Limited, The Glasshouse, 49a Goldhawk Road, London W12 8QP

Here We Go copyright © 2015 Caryl Churchill Limited

Caryl Churchill has asserted her right to be identified as the author of this work

Front cover image: Vangelis Paterakis

Designed and typeset by Nick Hern Books
Printed in Great Britain by Mimeo Ltd, Huntingdon, Cambridgeshire PE29 6XX

A CIP catalogue record for this book is available from the British Library

ISBN   978 1 84842 519 4

Woodland
CARBON
www.woodlandcarbon.co.uk
NICK HERN BOOKS
Printed on Carbon Captured paper

Here We Go was first performed in the Lyttelton auditorium of the National Theatre, London, on 27 November 2015 (previews from 25 November). The cast was as follows:

Madeline Appiah
Susan Engel
Patrick Godfrey
Hazel Holder
Joshua James
Amanda Lawrence
Stuart McQuarrie
Eleanor Matsuura
Alan Williams

Director	Dominic Cooke
Designer	Vicki Mortimer
Lighting Designer	Guy Hoare
Sound Designer	Christopher Shutt
Visual Effects	Chris Fisher
Company Voice Work	Jeannette Nelson
Staff Director	Rosemary McKenna
Stage Manager	Andrew Speed
Deputy Stage Manager	Fran Redvers-Jones

National Theatre

The National Theatre is dedicated to making the very best theatre and sharing it with as many people as possible.

We stage up to thirty productions at our South Bank home each year, ranging from re-imagined classics – such as Greek tragedy and Shakespeare – to modern masterpieces and new work by contemporary writers and theatre-makers. The work we make strives to be as open, as diverse, as collaborative and as national as possible. Much of that new work is researched and developed at the NT Studio: we are committed to nurturing innovative work from new writers, directors, creative artists and performers. Equally, we are committed to education, with a wide-ranging Learning programme for all ages in our new Clore Learning Centre and in schools and communities across the UK.

The National's work is also seen on tour throughout the UK and internationally, and in collaborations and co-productions with regional theatres. Popular shows transfer to the West End and occasionally to Broadway; and through the National Theatre Live programme, we broadcast live performances to 2,000 cinemas in fifty countries around the world. *National Theatre: On Demand in Schools* now makes three acclaimed, curriculum-linked productions free to stream on demand in every secondary school in the country. Online, the NT offers a rich variety of innovative digital content on every aspect of theatre.

We do all we can to keep ticket prices affordable and to reach a wide audience, and use our public funding to maintain artistic risk-taking, accessibility and diversity.

nationaltheatre.org.uk
Director   Rufus Norris
Executive Director   Lisa Burger

The number of actors can vary in different productions. Not fewer than three in the first scene and not more than eight – five or six is probably good. Age and gender can also be decided. The character in 'After' can be but needn't be the man whose funeral it is in the first scene. Same with 'Getting There', and the carer may or may not be someone we've met before.

This text went to press before the end of rehearsals and so may differ slightly from the play as performed.

1. HERE WE GO

The speeches at the end of the scene are to be inserted at random during the dialogue. There are ten – use as many as you need for each character to have one.

The place is a party after a funeral.

We miss him

of course

everyone

but his closest

because friendship was

wider range of acquaintance than anyone I've ever

gift

closeness

listened

and so witty I remember him saying

listened and understood

always seemed

though of course *are* you any wiser when you're older I feel sixteen all the time all he'd lived through

the war the war not so many people left who

and Spain even imagine

what how old

no he did

and he never actually joined the party because of what
they did to the anarchists so

not that he was an anarchist

unless sexually

well yes there

and is the third wife here are they all

in the red hat

isn't that the daughter?

no the big red

and is that her partner with the beard?

all the women seem

yes they all kiss but I wonder

except of course

she's keeping very quiet

love of his life

they say

though he was an old goat

of course

such charm was the thing

yes because he didn't look

oh when he was young

none of us can remember

well I can

of course

he was a vision at thirty

and photos photos have you seen there are some on the table in the

yes on a horse, about twelve

but his mind

yes his mind

extraordinary mind

literature of course but also

literature of France, Spain, Russia, every South American

physics, he had an extremely scientific

could have been

never fully

an mp in the fifties

I never knew

oh yes

which party

well obviously

yes but he was a libertarian

man of the left

always fell out

a bit too much of an individualist some might

just quarrelsome

but then he'd make it up with a bunch of flowers

I always remember a time he

and did you meet his friend Bill?

who isn't here or is he?

would we recognise?

heavy drinker

he put it away himself

but could always carry

champagne in hospital

so wonderful

never complained

well he did

terrible temper

I never saw

swore at the nurses

well I suppose anyone

yes pain

pain does change

horrible to see

morphine

can make you feel very happy, when I broke my pelvis

or sick

confused

sounded as if he was demented but of course we knew
it was

though he always did have a temper

I never saw

perhaps you didn't annoy

only the people who were closest

no, people he didn't know, cold-callers

van drivers

dogs

dogs?

he hated

never knew that

cats cats cats

yes what's going to happen

his daughter said she could take the old ginger tom but

in a flat?

cats like places of course more than people, they

your cat?

stopped being sick everywhere thank god, the vet's bills

and how are you keeping now you're

yes fantastic

wonderful job

New York in the morning so I can't stay too long I've got to

promotion

still hoping

painting

out of work so long now I

keeping busy

your new partner I hear

getting married

and you always said

yes but love when it really

yes

you don't quite expect

so happy for you

yes after all those

and we're expecting a baby in September but don't

so great

just close friends till

of course

another drink

have to remember I'm driving so

see all these people

yes because we hardly ever

and so many people I've never set eyes

all his different walks of

who've known him for sixty years

only met him last summer but he

talking to one of the carers

closer to him at the end I think than

well someone who washes

and wipes

you do love who you look after and who looks after you
like that's how with babies

or cats

all one way with cats

no stroking them reduces our

lovely service

favourite

but he wasn't a Christian surely or was it his

but what do you do?

plenty of people nowadays, pop songs, poems

yes despite everything he was rather

I don't think he cared, he's not the type who'd plan

no, plan their own service, oh dear

must keep an eye on the time

far to go?

came on the M23 and the roadworks at junction

go back through

long way round

stay overnight

long day tomorrow

I did cry

no I never actually have at a funeral

what sort of

self-pity and anger mainly I'm afraid, so

but that sort of lofty

uplifting

some bits of music

but not today's for me

no but the thought

yes hard to believe he's gone even though

it comes at you suddenly doesn't it

like stepping on a rake

I know after my mother

well parents of course are a different

not really

because then you're next

but you think your friend's still there in a different city and
not seeing them is

yes and then it hits you you'll never

and I find I can't remember voices

no not for long

we should all be recorded

please no, photographs are bad enough

oh but I love

let it go and just remember whatever we

the oddest things

can see him standing on one leg, I think it was in France
were you there

no I never went to that house just to the one in what was
that street?

very funny

he was

he could tell a joke

yes I can never remember

One of these is spoken by each of the characters directly to the audience. They should be inserted randomly into the previous dialogue in any order. The number of years later can be adjusted if necessary to make sense for the characters.

I die the next day. I'm knocked over by a motorbike crossing a road in North London. I think I can get over while the light's red but I'm looking for cars. I'm dead before the ambulance comes and it comes very quickly.

I die eleven years later. I have a heart attack swimming in the North Sea in January. I'd done it before all right.

I die thirty-eight years later of lung cancer. I hadn't realised before that you have different kinds of cancer depending on where it starts so you can have breast cancer in your brain, and I have lung cancer in my liver. I don't find the pain relief as helpful as I'd hoped.

I die five years later stabbed by an intruder. I keep a knife by the bed and when I brandish it he snatches it. He's shocked by the blood, he's saying sorry sorry and then I pass out.

I die twenty-six years later. I slip over on the icy steps going to put out the rubbish and break my hip, and my chest gets worse lying in bed. I have given up smoking but a bit late.

I die forty years later in my sleep, which is a relief. I was expecting to live to see the baby.

I die seven years later of a brain tumour. It takes a while for the doctors to pay attention to the headaches but maybe it would have spread anyway.

I die sixty-two years later. More and more things aren't working. They put pneumonia on the death certificate.

I die twenty-three years later after nine years of Alzheimer's. I don't know anyone who's there.

I die six months later. I hang myself. I should have thought about who'd find me.

2. AFTER

One person. Very fast.

Falling falling down the tunnel down the tunnel a tunnel a
light a train a tube train aaah coming to kill me

but I'm already dead is that right and ah here I am
arrived somewhere and hello is that grandpa?

surely not greater light and further shore no

but is this the pearly gates yes look actual pearls and that's
St Peter beard key

but I don't believe anything like

and it's gone is anyone there hello

there must be vast numbers of us that's a comfort far
more than the living

except of course there used to be fewer living at any one
time so maybe the living now equal all the dead could that
be but even so there are billions right back to cave and
where are they

oh there they are here we are I'm just a speck of sand in a
desert oh

or what is this are we all standing on the Isle of Wight it's
worse than the tube at rush hour I can't get my face away
from his back I don't want

ah that's better they've gone I'm on my own

I'm on my own

and what's happened to me what's going to happen I
always was afraid despite everything there'd be a
judgement and I'd be a goat not a sheep thinking of
those herds in North Africa where they're mixed together
and it can be hard to tell I understood the metaphor then
very good

and I think they don't emphasise hell these days but you
can't be sure because there's nothing kind about the
universe just rushing apart

and even our little place in it we evolved to belong has
hurricanes and cancer and is kind for some but often
unkind and they have to live with foul water or wake up in
dread and what would it be like to have to live your life as
someone obsessed with having sex with children or
wanting to kill what would you do with that

and it might not be fair to punish them but it may not be
fair because the universe isn't so who says god is if there is
one here somewhere

and hell used to be mediaeval tortures pincers and fire
and we thought god can't do that because no one would
do that

but we know people do just that sort of thing quite a lot so
maybe there is a hell of arms chopped off and piles of
bodies with bags on their heads and hanging upside down
ah why shouldn't I be one of the people who deserve that

if deserving comes into it it might be random

because I'm the rich camel who can't get through
compared to oh I know there's mega how reassuring
yachts but no I was comfortable comfortable in my life
chicken and a warm bed

and how much good did I very little because I was always
loving someone or organising something or looking at
trees or having a quiet sit-down with the paper and I'm
sorry I'm sorry

or is it purgatory do they have that still where it's burned
out of you not for ever yes I can feel it getting hotter the
blast of it on my

ridiculous I don't believe it of course never did that's not
happening there's plenty of other something completely

yes here comes aah his head's what a wild dog fox jackal
that's it not a mask he's

and that one's a bird ibis long curved sharp I'm sorry I'm
sorry

and here are the scales there's a feather in one pan so I
take out my heart and put it in the other and surely it
can't be light as a feather and if it weighs the pan down I
get thrown to that lion hippo crocodile and will I pass out
as I feel its hot breath sometimes people go into a swoon
of shock when an animal has them in its mouth National
Geographic probably and then I would really be dead and
gone I suppose

which ancient religion is this anyway Egypt

surely I must be in for something more Nordic

Thor with a thunderbolt

valhalla or is that just for war heroes yes there they are
sitting round the table drunk and roaring not my idea
of fun

and for illness or old age here's a blue black giantess
come to take me somewhere bleaker maybe a cold beach
with a wind I once went swimming I'd rather a warm
Greek white stones can I have that and is that Charon in
the boat I can get in wobble sit down and over the dark
river we go

I've always been scared of guard dogs so I hope Cerberus

and do I have to gibber with those bloodless dead did
Odysseus go to see them yes I can see him coming now
and here we are all stretching out our hands to him

but he won't do anything for me living so long after his
time and surely he's fictional anyway so how can he
help me get out of this hanging about and hanging
about for ever when I could be doing something like
going back and

walk haunt turn the room cold hear them talking and long
for someone to see me here I'm here my love can't you see
me hundreds of years still floating through walls I'm here
I'm here no I'm not a ghost story

going back and having another life my own life over again
like that movie and do it better of course because most of
the time I hardly noticed it going by and I used to look
back and think how careless I was when I was young I
never noticed and by then I was middle-aged and later I'd
look back and think *then* I never noticed

and another go would be welcome

but nobody suggests they do that in real life real death not
another go as yourself another go as somebody else or of
course some*thing* else

and have I lived the sort of life that would get me one step
up to be a happier better person one true love maybe I
deserve to paint or

no not be in power hate to be a president king general
imagine how terrible that might be a punishment of
course a step down

or I might have to sleep in the street yes I'm walking
miles with a heavy sick child I'm so depressed I can't put
on my socks

but I might not be human a bird a bird everyone wants to
fly oh a kestrel can I be a kestrel yes I can see every blade
of grass and a mouse drop on the mouse but I might be
the mouse

I might be a rabid street dog foaming a cow up the ramp
to the slaughter

I'd rather be an endangered species some beautiful far far
anywhere oh

I might be an insect one of billions I am already one of
billions but trillions

a locust eating and eating do they feel joy do they just eat
or maybe a flea blood and the amazing jump

oh I don't want to be the caterpillar the wasp lays an egg
in and it hatches and consumes from inside

but surely that's not a belief I've ever I've never

and I wouldn't be me this one I've been doesn't remember others it's extinction of me even if I'm part of some cosmic whatsit drop gone back to the ocean no

and of course all the bits of my body are on their way now breaking down into smaller and smaller rather disgusting at first but into the daisies

or did they have me cremated how odd I don't know in which case it's all gone up in smoke leaving just those gritty ashes that might be partly someone else's I'm not sure how particular they are at the crem when they sweep it out

but anyway all the chemicals atoms neutrons from stars on their way because the energy's still all there

but not my energy like 'oh I'm so tired today I've got no energy' now I've really got no energy it's somewhere else like before I was born

all those atoms are somewhere else

and you're just a thing that happens like an elephant or a daffodil

and there you all are for a short time

that's how it's put together for a short time

and oddly you are actually are one of those

and it goes on and on and you're used to it and then suddenly

3. GETTING THERE

A very old or ill person and a carer.

The old/ill person is in nightclothes and is helped by the carer to get dressed, slowly and with difficulty because of pain and restricted movement.

Then to get undressed and back into nightclothes.

Then to get dressed.

Then to get undressed and back into nightclothes.

Then to get dressed…

for as long as the scene lasts.

End.

Other works by Caryl Churchill, published by Nick Hern Books

Light Shining in Buckinghamshire
Traps
Cloud Nine
Icecream
Mad Forest
The Skriker
Thyestes (translated from Seneca)
Hotel
This is a Chair
Blue Heart
Far Away
A Number
A Dream Play (translated from Strindberg)
Drunk Enough to Say I Love You?
Bliss (translated from Olivier Choinière)
Seven Jewish Children – a play for Gaza
Love and Information
Ding Dong the Wicked

Collections

Plays: Three
    A Mouthful of Birds (with David Lan)
    Icecream
    Mad Forest
    Lives of the Great Poisoners (with Orlando Gough and Ian Spink)
    The Skriker
    Thyestes

Plays: Four
    Hotel
    This is a Chair
    Blue Heart
    Far Away
    A Number
    A Dream Play (translated from Strindberg)
    Drunk Enough to Say I Love You?

Shorts
    Lovesick
    Abortive
    Not Not Not Not Not Enough Oxygen
    Schreber's Nervous Illness
    The Hospital at the Time of the Revolution
    The Judge's Wife
    The After-Dinner Joke
    Seagulls
    Three More Sleepless Nights

Other Titles in this Series